Shakespearean Music
in the
Plays and Early Operas

AMS PRESS

NEW YORK

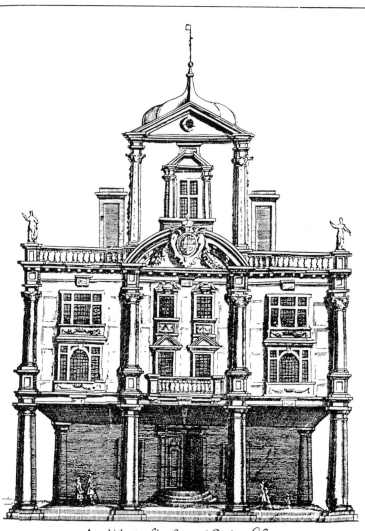

Amphitheatra *sile, et Spectacula Barbara Cæsar:*
Non coeunt Nudi, non Aper, Ursa, Leo.
Nos Mites colimus Musas, lenivit Amorq3
Prælia; cum nostro est Incola Marte Venus.
Quosq3 ferunt olim Thalamo cepisse, Theatro
Ludentes unà cernat Apollo Deos.

EXTERIOR OF WREN'S THEATRE
(DORSET GARDENS, 1674)

Shakespearean Music in the Plays and Early Operas

By
Sir Frederick Bridge
C.V.O., M.A., Mus.Doc.

*King Edward Professor of Music in the University
of London; Emeritus Organist of Westminster
Abbey; Gresham Professor of Music*

1923
London & Toronto
J. M. Dent & Sons Ltd.
New York: E. P. Dutton & Co.

Library of Congress Cataloging in Publication Data

Bridge, Sir Frederick, 1844-1924.
  Shakespearean music in the plays and early operas.

  Reprint of the 1923 ed. published by J. M. Dent, Lon-
don; E. P. Dutton, New York.
  "Musical appendix": p.
  1. Shakespeare, William, 1564-1616—Knowledge—Music.
I. Title.
ML80.S5B8   1975   782.8'3'0942   75-153307
ISBN 0-404-07808-7

ML
80
.S5
B8
1975

Reprinted with permission of J. M. Dent & Sons, Ltd.,
London, England

From the edition of 1923, London
First AMS edition published in 1975
Manufactured in the United States of America

AMS PRESS INC.
NEW YORK, N. Y. 10003

FOREWORD

SHAKESPEARE'S dramatic works have been the theme of endless books and articles by eminent scholars. The desire to secure a really correct version of the poet's lines has occupied the minds and talents of a multitude of writers, with the result that we are furnished with various editions differing very much from the older publications, but which are no doubt much more true to the original text.

The important place which music holds in Shakespeare's works is well known. In nearly all his plays provision is made for music—both instrumental and vocal.

Surely we ought if possible to get at the correct version of the music, and so to let this branch of Shakespeare's art be in keeping with the literary work.

I have for a long time kept this idea in mind, and have done my best when performing or writing about the music of Shakespeare's plays to give correct versions. It is the result of these studies which I have been persuaded to put into print, and which I hope may be welcome to all lovers of the poet.

CLOISTERS,
  WESTMINSTER ABBEY,
    May, 1923.

ACKNOWLEDGMENTS

THE thanks of the Author are hereby tendered to the Master of Magdalene College, Cambridge (A. C. Benson, Esq., C.V.O.), and to O. F. Morshead, Esq. (Librarian), for the facsimile of Hamlet's Soliloquy from the Pepysian Library. Also to the authorities of the Bodleian and Christ Church, Oxford, for permission to photograph the tablature parts (Citterne and Pandora) of " O Mistresse Mine." To the authorities of the Examination Schools, Oxford, for permission to reproduce the portraits of Matthew Locke and Dr. John Wilson. To E. F. Knapp-Fisher, Esq., Receiver-General of Westminster Abbey, for the photograph of Wilson's Grave and Banister's Tablet, to the Committee of the Garrick Club for the portrait of Betterton, to Messrs. Novello and Co. for the picture of the Shakespearean Band, and to Miss C. Stainer, Mr. Charles Stainer, and Mr. W. Barclay Squire for kind help in various ways.

CONTENTS

LIST OF ILLUSTRATIONS

SHAKESPEAREAN MUSIC

IN THE PLAYS AND EARLY OPERAS

CHAPTER I

SHAKESPEARE'S KNOWLEDGE OF MUSIC

SHAKESPEARE'S frequent tributes to the power of music, his apt use of musical terms and his many allusions to musical instruments, are, of course, well known.[1] We do not know anything of Shakespeare's intercourse with contemporary musicians, but there were many good composers and theoretical writers hard at work during Shakespeare's time, and it is certain he had knowledge of these men and their works and made good use of it. Of course, in those days music was an important branch of education, as important as Latin or Fencing. The story told in Morley's *Plaine and Easie Introduction to Practical Musike* illustrates this rather well. A young man is describing his unfortunate experience at an evening party of the period:

> Supper being ended, and music-books, *according to custom*, being brought to the table, the mistress of the house presented me with a part, earnestly requesting me to sing. But when, after many excuses, I protested unfeignedly that I could not, every one began to wonder, yea, some whispered to others demanding how I was brought up!

Now, what apparently was expected of a " well-brought-up " young man—one who would fulfil the conditions of

---

[1] For a complete list of quotations and admirable explanation see Dr. Naylor's book, *Shakespeare and Music* (J. M. Dent and Sons Ltd.). Also *Shakespeare in Music*, by Louis C. Elson (David Nutt).

Peacham's *Compleat Gentleman* so far as music was concerned—was that he should take part, at first sight, in a madrigal (the great vocal composition of the period) possibly in five or six parts, and to sing not from a score but from a single part—possibly also without bars; and because he had to " confess unfeignedly" that he could not, he was looked upon as one who had been badly " brought up." I am afraid our present standard of musical education is hardly up to what was required in those days!

The prevalent study of music in Elizabethan times, and the use made of it by the upper classes in their houses— with their " chest of viols "—and the itinerant vendors of merchandise in London (as evidenced by the remarkable " Old Cryes " which I have had the good fortune to unearth), would make it advisable for any clever dramatist to introduce lyrics and instrumental music into his plays. And this is what Shakespeare did to a remarkable extent. It will be seen later on that, in some cases, he took lyrics with their settings which were popular, and inserted them, with some alteration of the words, in various plays. It was at one time thought that not a single note of the music originally written to Shakespeare's plays was to be found. Professor Edward Taylor (one of my predecessors as Gresham Professor of Music) said in one of his lectures: " It is much to be regretted that the original music to all Shakespeare's dramatic songs should have perished. No musical history with which I am acquainted contains any record of them, and no traces of their existence have I been able to discover." We are in a better position now. The access to great libraries and the careful cataloguing of their contents have, with other things, enabled us to acquire some of these most interesting and valuable treasures, and it is to this music which formed part of the earliest representation of the plays, and also to the music written for Shakespeare's works later on in the seventeenth century, that I propose to direct attention.

Before, however, treating of the songs, I think it may be of interest to give a few of the more important allusions to (a) Musical Instruments and (b) Musical Form.

My words on these points will be brief, because the subject has been really exhausted in the two books to which I have referred in a note on page 1.

A curious allusion is to be found in *The Merchant of Venice*, where Shylock speaks of

> The vile squeaking of the wry-neck'd fife.

This has been much discussed by Shakespearean students. C. Knight says " there is some doubt whether the ' wry-neck'd fife ' is here the instrument or the musician." Later on we shall have an example of the trumpet player being addressed (by Ajax) as " Thou Trumpet." Boswell gives a quotation from Barnaby Rich's *Aphorisms* (1618) which is very much to the point : "A fife is a wry-neck't musician, for he always looks away from the instrument." Dr. Naylor, however, gives the following explanation, which seems to settle the matter.

Mercenne (born 1588) says that the fife is the same as the Tibia Helvetica, which was simply a small edition of the Flauto Traverso, or German flute. That is, the fife of those days was much the same as the modern fife, with the usual six holes and a big hole near the stopped end where the breath was applied. The instrument was therefore held *across* (" traverso ") the face of the player, whose head would be turned sideways, and hence comes Shylock's description of it as the " wry-neck'd fife."

I am bound to say some authorities do not accept this. Mr. J. Finn, who plays many of the old instruments, tells me it is not necessary for the player to turn his head awry! Sometimes I have wondered if the expression " wry-neck'd " had anything to do with the *bird* wryneck. This is described as " a small bird allied to the woodpecker, so called from the singular manner in which, when surprised, it turns its head over its shoulder." Now there is an instrument of Shakespeare's time—a cornet—which has a curve in it, and when held by the player " looks round towards his shoulder." It also, as regards tone, suits the epithet "vile" a little better than the harmless fife. But I do not press this. The whole subject has been so often discussed, it seems impossible to be certain if Shakespeare really meant the fife or made a mistake and confused it with the cornet.

In *Hamlet* we find an interesting reference to the recorder. It is in the passage where Hamlet, rebuking Guildenstern, calls for the recorders.

Oh, the recorders, let me see one. . . . Will you play upon this pipe?
Guild. My lord, I cannot.
Ham. I pray you.
Guild. Believe me, I cannot.
Ham. I do beseech you.
Guild. I know no touch of it, my lord.
Ham. 'Tis as easy as lying: govern these ventages with your finger and thumb, give it breath with your mouth, and it will discourse most eloquent music. Look you, these are the stops.
Guild. But these cannot I command to any utterance of harmony; I have not the skill.
Ham. Why, look you now, how unworthy a thing you make of me! You would play upon me: you would seem to know my stops: you would pluck out the heart of my mystery: you would sound me from my lowest note to the top of my compass: and there is much music, excellent voice, in this little organ: yet cannot you make it speak. 'Sblood, do you think I am easier to be played on than a pipe? Call me what instrument you will, though you can fret me, yet you cannot play upon me.
Hamlet, Act III. Sc. ii.

There is a curious point in this speech of Hamlet to

which I will allude for a moment: "You can fret me."
This is an allusion to the frets which were found upon the
viols and other stringed instruments of the period, and
which are to be found even now upon the guitar. They
were divisions upon the neck of the instrument, showing
where the fingers should be placed. It is not easy to see
the connection between this word and the recorder, which
was a wind instrument having "ventages" or air-holes
upon which the fingers were placed. The stops are the
ventages or air-holes.

In *Troilus and Cressida* we find the power of the warlike
trumpet thus invoked by King Agamemnon:

> Give with thy trumpet a loud note to Troy,
> Thou dreadful Ajax! that the appalled air
> May pierce the head of the great combatant,
> And hale him hither.
> *Ajax.*   Thou trumpet, there's my purse.
> Now crack thy lungs, and split thy brazen pipe;
> Blow, villain, till thy spherèd bias cheek
> Outswell the colic of puff'd Aquilon:
> Come, stretch thy chest, and let thy eyes spout blood!
> Thou blow'st for Hector.
>   Act IV. Sc. v.

We may remark here that though Shakespeare did not certainly undervalue the penetrating power of the trumpet,
yet he shows an absence of knowledge of the proper method
of blowing. The "spherèd bias cheek" would suggest
that the player distended his cheeks, whereas all who have
ever tried to make a sound—say upon a post-horn—
know that this method produces no result, but that the
lips and tongue are the important factors concerned. But,
of course, Shakespeare here makes Ajax speak with the
tongue of a braggart, and probably the demand for an
exaggerated effort on the part of the trumpet is in keeping
with the whole speech. The "sennet" alluded to in *Macbeth*

and other plays meant a flourish of trumpets announcing the approach of some important personage. The term " broken-music," as in *Troilus and Cressida,* probably denoted the music of stringed instruments such as lutes and guitars, because the sound of these instruments cannot be sustained at will.

Another explanation is that " broken music " was any combination of instruments of different kinds. I confess I think the first explanation is the more likely.

An example of Shakespeare's knowledge of musical form is

> For on that ground I'll make a holy descant.
> *Richard III.,* Act. III. Sc. vii.

This refers to the well-known practice of composers writing upon a " ground-bass," *i.e.* a short musical phrase repeated over and over again, the harmony which was superposed on the ground being the " holy descant."

Another quotation may be permitted as showing Shakespeare's knowledge of the material from which catgut for the viol strings was made :

> Now, divine air ! Now is his soul ravished ! Is it not strange that sheep's guts should hale souls out of men's bodies?
> *Much Ado About Nothing,* Act II. Sc. iii.

CHAPTER II

THE ACCOMPANIMENT OF THE SONGS. THE SINGERS

BEFORE commenting upon the songs, it will be well to explain the way in which they were accompanied, and also consider the people who sang them.

The original accompaniments to the songs in the plays were not, of course, written for a *pianoforte*! the lute and the bass viol were the usual instruments, and it is the accompaniments written for them which I have as far as possible adopted.

The lute was a large instrument, plucked by the fingers and not played with a bow. It has long been obsolete and few people can now make much use of it. It was a difficult instrument to play and to keep in tune, and an old author says: " If a lutenist attains the age of eighty you may be sure he has spent sixty years of his life tuning his instrument, and I have been told that in Paris it cost as much to keep a lute in order as would keep a horse! "

Another old author gives this advice for preserving the instrument. " You shall do well, even when you lay it by in the day-time, to put it into a bed that is constantly used, between the rug and the blanket." He adds that there is a danger of people sitting upon the bed and smashing the lute, and that he had lost two or three lutes in that way!

With regard to the singers. Although some of the actors may have sung, yet there are examples of singers being introduced who have nothing to do with the action of the play. For instance, in *As You Like It,* the song " It was a Lover and his Lass " is sung by two pages apparently introduced for the purpose. In *The Merchant of Venice* the song " Tell me where is Fancy bred " is preceded by the stage direction, " Music, while Bassanio comments on the caskets to himself," and the song has a " burden " (or chorus), " Ding, dong, bell," which is directed to be sung by all. In the infancy of the Theatre companies of boy actors were very general. The boys of St. Paul's and the Chapel Royal constantly acted before the Court and nobility. It seems probable that the theatrical establishments of royal and noble persons were in a way attached to their chapels, and in order to ensure a supply of good voices boys were actually pressed into the service, being taken by force even from other establishments. An account of such a case, written by a boy who attained some considerable distinction in after life—Thomas Tusser, author of the *Five Hundred Points of Good Husbandry* (born in the reign of Henry VIII.) —may be of interest. Tusser was a boy at Wallingford in Berkshire and taken by force, for his voice, by a pressgang. The poem is a preface to his book.

> What robes! how bare! what colledge fare!
> What bread how stale! What penny ale!
> Then Wallingford how wert thou abhor'd
>   Of silly boies!
>
> Thence for my voice I must (no choice)
> Away of force like posting horse,
> For sundry men had placards then
>   Such child to take:
> The better brest,[1] the lesser rest,
> To serve the queere,[2] now there, now here,
> For time so spent, I may repent,
>   And sorrow make.

[1] If a boy had a good voice he was said to have a good " brest."   [2] *I.e.* quire.

But marke the chance, myself to 'vance,
By friendship's lot to Paule's I got;
So found I grace a certain space
    Still to remain
With Redford [1] there, the like no where
For cunning such and vertue much
By whom some part of musicke art
    So did I gaine.

From Paule's I went, to Eaton sent
To learn streightwaies the Latin phraies
Where fiftie stripes given to mee
    At once I had
For fault but small or none at all,
It came to pass thus beat I was;
See, Udall,[2] see the mercie of thee
    To me poore lad.

From London hence, to Cambridge thence
With thankes to thee, O Trinitie,
That to thy hall, so passing all,
    I got at last.

It will be seen later on, in connection with the production of the early operas, that the boys and men of the Royal Chapel were constantly employed in the performances.

[1] Redford was the Organist.   [2] Udall was the Headmaster.

CHAPTER III

CONTEMPORARY SONGS

THE settings of Shakespearean lyrics which were published in his lifetime are, I am afraid, only two—" O Mistresse Mine " (*Twelfth Night*) and " It was a Lover and his Lass " (*As You Like It*). They are both delightful specimens, and worthy of being presented in a correct form. Many versions of them have appeared from time to time, some dreadful mutilations of the original, and in some cases very fairly correct so far as the melody is concerned. Like many other things connected with Shakespeare, the original printed copies are extremely rare, and in the case of " O Mistresse Mine " not quite complete. But I think I have been able to restore both these beautiful songs to something very near the originals. The earliest copy of " O Mistresse Mine " is in a very rare collection of airs arranged by Morley for a small band of six instruments, published in 1599. The title is very quaint : " The First Booke of Consort Lessons, made by divers exquisite Authors for six Instruments to play together, the Treble-Lute, the Pandora, the Citterne, the Bass-Viol, the Flute and Treble-Viol. Neatly set forth at the cost and charges of a gentleman, for his private pleasure, and for divers others his friendes which delight in Musick."

One would like to know who the gentleman was who paid the cost and charges of this little collection—and if he knew Shakespeare!

WILLIAM BYRDE

This " O Mistresse Mine " is the most interesting thing in the collection. A proof of its popularity is the fact that the air is also found in the Fitzwilliam *Virginal Book,* and used as a theme upon which five variations were written by the celebrated William Byrde, a contemporary of Shakespeare.

I have chosen Morley's version rather than Byrde's. The latter was merely an arrangement of the air with variations for the virginal. The words fit Morley's simple version much better than Byrde's, but an accidental to the seventh note of the air is omitted by Morley. This is evidently a printer's error, as the citterne and pandora parts prove the correct note is as Byrde wrote it (C sharp).

Dr. Burney is very sarcastic in commenting on this little collection, particularly in reference to the fact that Morley dedicated the volume to the Lord Mayor. He says:

Master Morley, supposing perhaps that the harmony which was to be heard through the clattering of knives, forks, spoons and plates, with the jingling of glasses and clamorous conversation of a City feast, need not be very accurate or refined, was not very nice in setting parts to these tunes, which are so far from correct that almost any one of the City waits would (in musical cant) have vamped as good an accompaniment.

This is very smart, but I am convinced it is not true. At any rate, the accompaniment of this song (which is Morley's harmony) is perfectly good and appropriate. I do not believe Burney ever saw a complete set of the parts, and so never heard the harmony at which he jibes. Even now we have not a complete set of parts, and I am certain there was no such thing in Burney's time.

As I have already said, this charming song has been

much mutilated. The arrangement which I now give
was a matter of some difficulty. The melody I took
from the viol part of Morley's arrangement for the band
of six. This was the only part in the library of the Royal
College of Music. I went to the British Museum with the
confident hope of finding the other parts. Alas! like everything else concerning Shakespeare, the complete parts are
not forthcoming. There was only one part—that for the
flute or recorder. However, this furnished me with an
inner part to the melody and I had to supply the bass myself.
This I did, and it was printed in a small collection
of Shakespeare's songs.[1]   A little later I was fortunate
enough to recover another of the missing parts in the
Bodleian Library. This was the citterne part, a small instrument with strings and played with a plectrum. This
part consists of chords of three or four notes, and I at
once recognised the fact that I should have to compare
the bass and the harmony which I had supplied with the
chords now for the first time revealed to me! I was almost
inclined to let the newly-discovered part go back again to
its quiet resting-place. But I determined to risk having
made some mistakes. As a result I am able to say my part
differed from the original harmony in very few places. And
so we have now a really correct copy. I may add that since
all this happened another of the missing parts—that for the
pandora, a species of lute—has turned up in the library of
Christ Church, Oxford, and also a flute part. This is not
of very great importance, as the part also consists of chords
which agree mostly with the citterne part, but it supplies
a good deal of the real bass. So we now only want the
parts for lute and bass viol, which may yet be found in

[1] Most of the songs mentioned in this book can be had in a complete form—
in a small volume, edited by the Author and published at Novello's, entitled
Songs from Shakespeare: the earliest known settings.

O MISTRESSE MINE

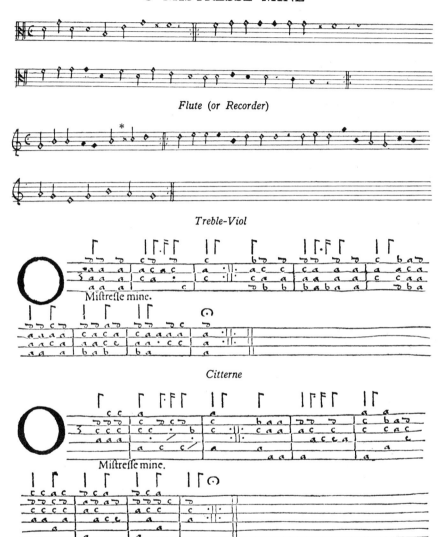

Flute (or Recorder)

Treble-Viol

Miſtreſſe mine.

Citterne

Miſtreſſe mine.

Pandora

MORLEY'S INSTRUMENTAL PARTS OF "O MISTRESSE MINE"

* This sharp is wanting in the original, but is proved to be a printer's error.

some unexplored library, and there is no doubt that we have the harmony quite satisfactorily correct.[1]

I may add that at the Musicians Company's Exhibition at Fishmongers' Hall some years ago this exquisite bit of Shakespearean music was played by a body of six amateurs, under the direction of the Rev. F. W. Galpin, on the six instruments for which Morley scored it, and with delightful effect. I am able to give a picture of the players taken on this occasion.

By the kindness of the authorities of the Bodleian Library of Christ Church, Oxford, I have been able to obtain fac-similes of the citterne and pandora parts; and have also obtained those for the viol and flute, which cannot fail to be interesting. The pandora and citterne parts are in tablature. A copy of the song in modern notation will be found on page 77 of the Appendix.

" It was a Lover and his Lass "

This song was written to Shakespeare's words and is the composition of Morley, who edited the collection in which we find " O Mistresse Mine." Morley was a very prominent London musician, and must certainly have known Shakespeare. The Rev. Joseph Hunter, in his book, *Illustrations of the Life of Shakespeare* (1845), published a document which he had discovered which gives us a bit of interesting information concerning Shakespeare and Morley. Morley lived in the parish of St. Helen's, Bishopsgate, between 1596 and 1601. Shakespeare also resided in that parish soon after his arrival in London, but in the autumn of 1596, Sir Sidney Lee tells us, " he migrated across the Thames to Southwark. . . . His name had been placed on the roll of ' subsidy men,' or taxpayers, for St. Helen's Parish,

---

[1] In the version printed in the Appendix I have corrected the harmony which was not correct in my early edition. This I have been able to do from the citterne and pandora parts.

Treble-Viol   Flute (Recorder)   Citterne   Pandora   Lute   Bass-Viol

MORLEY'S BAND FOR HIS ARRANGEMENT OF "O MISTRESSE MINE"

and his personal property valued for fiscal purposes at £5. But the collection of taxes in the City of London worked sluggishly and for three years they put no pressure on the dramatist, and Shakespeare left Bishopsgate without discharging the debt." However, later on the revenue officer of St. Helen's claimed the first instalment, and the *Roll of Assessment* which Mr. Hunter quotes gives the name of William Shakespeare and also that of Thomas Morley. Both poet and musician were assessed for the same amount —both appealed, and it seems as if both paid. The years which Morley lived in Bishopsgate, in which he was thus brought into contact with Shakespeare, are the years in which he published the two Shakespeare songs, "O Mistresse Mine" and "It was a Lover." All this tends to prove the intimacy of the two men, and possibly the names of many well-to-do men on the *Roll of Assessment* may include the name of the gentleman who paid the cost and charges of the publication of "O Mistresse Mine."

It certainly looks as if Morley well knew the poet, and it is, as I have said, to him we owe the only musical settings of Shakespeare which appeared in his lifetime.

The song was contained in "The First Book of Ayres or Little Short Songs to sing and play to the Lute with the Bass Viol, by Thomas Morley, 1600."

An original printed copy (and, I rather think, the only copy existing) of the song, if I remember rightly, I saw in a great collection of Shakespearean books which I understood formed part of Mr. Halliwell-Phillipps' library, and which was for a time placed in a City safe deposit. It was from this book I made my copy of the melody, and the bass, which was furnished me by Mr. Woolridge, the editor of the new edition of Chappell's *Popular Music of the Olden Time*, was, I understood, from the same source. Mr. Woolridge has inserted a version in his edition of

"Chappell," but he has rather varied the bass as given to me, and I feel certain the bass-viol part is in one important place transferred to an inner part, with a considerable loss of effect. I fear this valuable book has gone to America, and so far I have failed to come across another copy. There is one little error in the words of this song which has been constantly made. It occurs even in such a well-known collection as Palgrave's *Golden Treasury*. The lines are in verse three:

> This Carol they began that hour
> How that a life was but a flower.

In the second line Palgrave (as others have done and as composers have set) writes, "How that life" instead of "How that a life." The incorrect version does not fit the music unless one of the melody notes is omitted.

The dialogue which introduces the song has suggested to some that Shakespeare contemplated a trio between the two Pages and Touchstone, who asks for the song and is requested to "sit i' the middle." I have also seen an ingenious attempt to make the song into a canon for two voices, the arranger deriving his idea of this interpretation of the song from the remarks, "Shall we clap into 't roundly?" and the reply, "I' faith, i' faith, and both in a tune, like two gipsies on a horse." (I ought, perhaps, to explain that in a canon one voice starts *behind the other* but singing the same tune, and we may imagine that two gipsies on a horse sat one behind the other.) However, I will not attempt to prove this, nor do I think it a correct view.

The version in the original edition of Chappell's *Music of the Olden Time* is very incorrect, some of the melody notes being changed and the bass modernised and hardly recognisable.

The dialogue between the two Pages and Touchstone is very amusing, and shows Shakespeare's knowledge of vocalists (both amateur and professional), who so often excuse themselves on the ground of " being hoarse."

Enter two Pages. (*They meet Touchstone.*)

First Page. Well met, honest gentleman.
Touch. By my troth, well met. Come, sit, sit, and a song.
Second Page. We are for you: sit i' the middle.
First Page. Shall we clap into 't roundly, without hawking or spitting
   or saying we are hoarse, which are the only prologues to a bad voice?
Second Page. I' faith, i' faith: and both in a tune, like two gipsies
   on a horse.   Act V. Scene iii.

The original settings of " Where the bee sucks " and " Full fathom five " are fortunately preserved to us. These were apparently not published until thirty or forty years after the poet's death. Of them I shall speak later. There is one charming song, the correct musical version of which has only been recovered during the last few years. It is the song " Whoop! do me no harm," which was among the wares of the pedlar Autolycus in *The Winter's Tale,* and which is referred to by the maid-servant when she mentions " he hath songs for man or woman." This song was unknown to me until it was pointed out by the late Dr. Southgate as being one of the airs in a valuable seventeenth-century book of viol da gamba pieces, which is now in the Henry Watson Library at Manchester. The original words are, unfortunately, not forthcoming, but the words I have set to the tune were supplied from an ancient source by Dr. Southgate. They are to be found in *Westminster Drollery* (1672), in a ballad of " Johnny and Jenny," which has evidently been attached to the melody. The " burden " shows it must have been set to the old tune, and the little rush up of three notes set to the word " Whoop " proves this—it suits the word to a nicety. It is a beautiful specimen of old melody, and probably existed and was popular as a ballad before Shakespeare's time—

E

or the pedlar would hardly have carried it about. The accompaniment is an adaptation of the gamba book harmony. The delightful way in which the instrument imitates the singer in the second part of the song will not escape notice.

A facsimile of the music as it appears in the Manchester Corporation book will be of interest as showing the tablature employed for viol da gamba music. A verse of the song in modern notation is given on page 80 of Appendix.

WHOOP! DO ME NO HARM
From the Manchester Viol da Gamba Music

The next song to be considered is one of the most beautiful: " Willo Willo "—Desdemona's song in *Othello*. This is an example of a song, words and music, undoubtedly written before Shakespeare's day, and which he introduced in *Othello*, altering the words to suit a female character. This delightful setting has been sadly mutilated by various editors, particularly by their omitting the rests which separate the earlier phrases. The lute may have echoed the voice at this point, and I have endeavoured to follow this idea in the arrangement of the accompaniment. The melody is from a MS. in the British Museum, and is of such interest that I have decided to give it in facsimile. There is no evidence as to the composer of words or music.

WILLO WILLO

The earliest known setting, from the MS. in the British Museum.[1]

[1] A modern version of this and other songs in the book is published by Novello & Co., edited by Sir F. Bridge.

CHAPTER IV

SONGS APPEARING AT A LATER PERIOD

WE come now to one of the most interesting of Shake-speare's songs. Who does not know Arne's setting of "Where the bee sucks"? Who would not like to hear the setting which Shakespeare heard? The composition I am about to consider is, I have no doubt, the original setting. It is contained, together with "Full fathom five," in a work entitled "Cheerful Ayres or Ballads, first composed for one single voice, and since set for three voices by John Wilson, Dr. in Music, Professor of Music in the University of Oxford, being the first essay of printed music ever seen in Oxford."

It was for a long time considered that Dr. Wilson had composed the whole of these "Cheerful Ayres," amounting in all to about seventy. Supposing this to be the case, these settings of Shakespeare's words would be full of interest. Wilson was born in 1594 and died in 1673, "aged seventy-eight years, ten months and seventeen days." I am able to quote these particulars from the fact that Wilson is buried near my study window in the Cloisters of Westminster Abbey, and I thus have the inscription on his gravestone well imprinted on my memory. Wilson was a contemporary of Shakespeare, and indeed by some has been identified as the "Jacke Wilson" whose name appears in the First Folio in connection with the song "Sigh no more, ladies." As I have said, Wilson was born in 1594,

Dr. John Wilson

and therefore he could not have sung the song at the first production in 1599, as he was then but five years of age. Of course he may have sung it at a later time, and his name might have therefore appeared in the First Folio, when he was about twenty-nine years of age.

Nothing is really known of him until 1636, when he was appointed a Gentleman of the Chapel Royal. It is suggested that in early life he was a member of the Burbages' Company to which Shakespeare belonged.

Be this as it may, he occupied a prominent position in the musical world, and would, no doubt, be familiar with Shakespeare's plays and the music which was set to the lyrics found in them. Now, curiously enough, to those two songs ("Where the bee sucks" and "Full fathom five") the name of R. Johnson is appended in Wilson's book. If Wilson had himself composed these songs he would hardly have put another man's name to them! Musicians do not do that! Robert Johnson was a contemporary of Shakespeare and has always been credited with having written music for the plays. I think there can be no doubt that Wilson merely rearranged these songs for three voices, retaining the original melody with which he was well acquainted.

"Where the bee sucks" is a delightful little song, as bright and tuneful—though, of course, much more simple than Arne's popular setting. Indeed, Arne seems, like a busy bee himself, to have sucked a little of this very flower. He must have known it. At any rate he began his setting with the same three notes we find in Johnson, only in a different key. The change to triple time at the words "Merrily, merrily shall I live now" is particularly effective. In "Full fathom five" we have a setting of a more sombre character but one full of dignity. "A sea-change" is admirably expressed, as also is the passage "Hark! now I

WHERE THE BEE SUCKS

The earliest known version

Cantus Primus.

R. Johnſon.

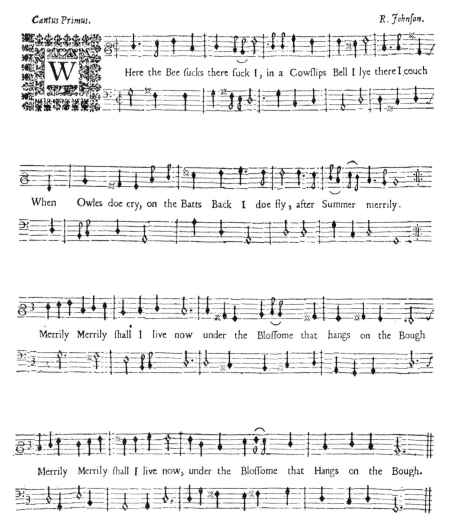

Here the Bee ſucks there ſuck I, in a Cowſlips Bell I lye there I couch

When Owles doe cry, on the Batts Back I doe fly, after Summer merrily.

Merrily Merrily ſhall I live now under the Bloſſome that hangs on the Bough

Merrily Merrily ſhall I live now, under the Bloſſome that Hangs on the Bough.

hear them, ding, dong, bell." I give a facsimile of Wilson's edition of "Where the bee sucks."

Before we leave Wilson I must mention one or two points of interest which I glean from the book of "Cheerful Ayres" already mentioned. The work was, as already stated, the first music book printed at Oxford, and there are many laudatory verses (as was the custom) addressed to the author by his admiring friends, and printed with the volume.

In one we are told that the Oxford Music School had been until Wilson's time the School of Rhetoric.

> Your school did never so deserve its name
> As since your ravishing rhetoric thither came.

In another we are told King Charles's opinion of Wilson's music " when some of these Ayres were performed to him by Dr. Wilson, Mr. Low and others ":

> I do not wonder that the King did call,
> " Wilson, there's more words, let's hear them all."
> Such was your skill that what the rest o' the Court
> Perhaps thought long, judicious ears thought short.
> Excellent Artist! whose sweet strains devour
> Time swift as they and make days seem an hour.
> But what need more—since 'tis enough to tell
> But this, King Charles hath heard, and liked them well!

It may be added that King Charles is reported to have said, *apropos* of Wilson's performance on the lyra-viol, " He did wonders upon an inconsiderable instrument." His majesty played the viol da gamba, a more important instrument in his eyes, no doubt.

Another of the musician's friends prophesies undying fame for the professor. I am afraid this is hardly so. At least I can of my own knowledge tell of a little incident which goes to prove that Wilson is not so well known as one could wish. I have stated that he lies in the Cloisters of Westminster Abbey, and in the course of time the inscription on his gravestone became much worn by the feet of the many visitors to the Abbey. At the suggestion of a musical enthusiast the Dean and Chapter ordered the stone to be re-cut, and while the workman was carrying out his task, the gentleman who had got it done stood by and explained what a distinguished man lay beneath the stone : " Shakespeare's tenor, Professor of Music at Oxford, Gentleman of the Chapel Royal and a great composer," etc., etc.

The workman listened with interest, and then, pausing for a moment, exclaimed, " Ah! I wish I had know'd that when we took that there drain-pipe through him! "

Of course he meant through the grave, not, let us hope, through poor Wilson's body.

To what base uses we may return, Horatio! Why may not imagination trace the noble dust of Alexander, till he find it stopping a bung-hole?   *Hamlet*, Act V. Scene i.

Having said so much of Wilson, and seeing that we owe to him the preservation of the earliest settings of " Where the bee " and " Full fathom five," I must mention his own beautiful setting of " Take, O take those lips away." It has been said this was probably used upon the stage during the life-time of Shakespeare, but Wilson would be only about twenty when Shakespeare died, and I do not think it at all likely he wrote the song so early in life, but it is interesting as being the earliest known setting.

I am able to give a picture of Wilson's grave in the Cloisters of Westminster Abbey.

DR. JOHN WILSON'S GRAVE IN THE LITTLE CLOISTER, WESTMINSTER ABBEY

CHAPTER V

SOME CONTEMPORARY AIRS

I HAVE now come to the end of the more important of the songs which were composed in Shakespeare's life-time or which existed before his plays were written. There are, of course, a good many airs which have interest and which are to be found in various collections. Amongst these are "Heartsease," "Light-o'-love" and "Green Sleeves." There is something to be said about this latter song. It is twice mentioned in *The Merry Wives of Windsor*. In Act V. Scene v. Falstaff says, " Let the sky rain potatoes; let it thunder to the tune of ' Green Sleeves ' "; and Mrs. Ford says, " I would have sworn his disposition would have gone to the truth of his words; but they do no more adhere and keep place together than the Hundredth Psalm to the tune of ' Green Sleeves.' "

The tune is well known and has been very popular to the words " Which nobody can deny." But I have lately come upon a version of it which is undoubtedly of Shakespeare's time, and which differs very much from the accepted version, though one can trace points of similarity in both. The version I allude to occurs in a " Humorous Fancy " by William Cobbold, one of the contributors to *The Triumphs of Oriana*, and organist of Norwich Cathedral. This " Fancy " is one of a class of composition which has been quite overlooked by musicians. The " Fancy " for instruments is, of course, a well-known form, but the " Humorous Fancies " of which I speak were written for a quartet or quintet of viols with vocal music of four or five parts superimposed. The *Old Cryes of London* were made use of for some of these compositions (by Weelkes, Deering and Gibbons), and Cobbold has written a similar work which he entitles *New Fashions*. It is somewhat lengthy, and the vocal parts are almost entirely founded upon an old air called " Brownings," which is sung to lines devoted to many of the trades and professions of the time. A few quotations may not be unwelcome:

NEW FASHIONS

New fashions now do bear the sway
And fashions old are laid away.

The brewer proves by his good ale
That one thing soon is new and stale.

The tailor night and day takes pains
New fashions to invent for gains.

The drawer, with his works of price,
Can money draw with his device.

The complete air is sung by various voices in turn, and the above selection is followed—why, one cannot explain—by the old tune of " Green Sleeves," with its own particular words. Cobbold was born in 1560, dying in 1639, and was thus a contemporary of Shakespeare. This makes the version of " Green Sleeves " which he used somewhat interesting. Cobbold's version and the setting which is generally quoted will be found on page 79 of Appendix, and although in different time-measures the two are much alike. I confess to liking Cobbold's better than the well-known one!

Another Shakespearean tune is also inserted into this composition, " Peg o' Ramsey," a favourite song of Sir Toby Belch. This is a much better tune than either of the versions generally given. For this tune see page 80 of Appendix.

CHAPTER VI

THE MUSIC OF THE PLAYS AND THE OPERAS

WE have now to transfer our attention to a later period. During the Commonwealth the theatre was neglected, but in 1656 a beginning was made by the production of *The Siege of Rhodes*. Before considering this opera I will quote some admirable remarks of Dr. Wheatley in a paper read before the Samuel Pepys Club in 1904 on the subject of Davenant's operas, acted during later years of the Commonwealth. He says, " I propose to set before you a few notes on the remarkable attempts made near the end of the Protectorate to introduce some kind of musical entertainment, to be called an opera rather than a play, which was then a hated term.

" Cromwell seems to have come to the conclusion that the people required some sort of popular amusement. Bulstrode Whitelocke, Sergeant Maynard, and others supported this view, and owing to Whitelocke's acquaintance with Sir William Davenant, that well-known dramatist learned that he would be allowed, in spite of previous prohibition, to present a carefully arranged entertainment that should not greatly shock the sentiments of the people who were likely to attend.

" Davenant was very careful in his steps to attain his end (the production of an opera), and wrote to Thurloe, ' If moral representation may be allowed (being without obsceneness, profaneness and scandal) the first arguments may consist of the Spaniards' barbarous conquests in the West

Indies and their several cruelties there exercised upon the subjects of this nation.'

"Davenant wished to produce *The Siege of Rhodes*, but it was thought best to commence the new undertaking with a specially undramatic piece which would prepare the public for something of a more theatrical character. Therefore there was performed early in 1656 a curious piece entitled ' The First Day's Entertainment at Rutland House by Declamation and Musik after the manner of the Ancients. By Sir W. D.'

" The place of performance was a room built at the back of Rutland House, Aldersgate Street, near what is now Charterhouse Square, and the date of performance was the 23rd of May, 1656."

Dr. Wheatley quotes a most valuable account of the performance which is contained among the State Papers, from which I select a few points of interest: " The roome was narrow, at the end of which was a Stage and on either side two places railed in, purpled and guilt. The Curtayn, also, that drew before this was of cloth of gold and purple."

After the Prologue (which told them this was *but the narrow passage to the Elyzium theire Opera*) up came Diogenes and Aristophanes, the first against the opera, the other for it.

The music was by Henry Lawes[1] and Dr. Colman and Captain Cooke and Ned Coleman and his wife, and others. " It lasted an houre and a halfe and," an announcement said, " is to continue for ten days, by which time other declamations will be ready."

Dr. Wheatley says it was a witty and interesting production, but scarcely one to attract an audience. Pepys

[1] It is interesting to find Henry Lawes, the composer of the last and greatest of the masques, *Comus* (1634), contributing twenty-six years later to the music of the first real operatic attempt.

read it with pleasure, but does not say he had seen it. " With great mirth read Sir W. Davenant's two speeches in dispraise of London and Paris, by way of reproach one to another."

Davenant lays great stress upon what he calls " moral representation " as his object in producing the public divertissements. He makes Aristophanes express his own views as to this:

" I shall learn to avoid such presumption as must shamefully require your pardon, and will not treat of busy, but pleasant assemblies, and particularly of such as meet for recreation by moral representations "; adding, " But Diogenes is implacably offended at recreation. He would have you all housed like himself, and everyman stay at home in his tub! "

I have quoted Dr. Wheatley at great length because it is the most lucid and valuable explanation of the steps to introduce opera which I have ever met with. There is no doubt this led to the production of the first English opera, *The Siege of Rhodes*, which was produced shortly after 3rd September, 1566, the date when it appeared in print.

The Siege of Rhodes was a very great advance upon the " Entertainments," and Davenant seems to have spared no pains to make it a real operatic show. He had the best musicians, composers and actors, and the scenery was designed by Webb, pupil and executor of Inigo Jones.[1] There is no doubt this production was a remarkable event in stage history and in the history of opera, and Mr. Joseph Knight's claim for the distinction of *The Siege of Rhodes* as set forth in the *Dictionary of National Biography* is well founded. He wrote: " It is, in some respects, the most epoch-marking play in the language. It was sung ' Stilo Recitativo '

---

[1] It was revised, and a new second part added, and Pepys, in 1661, went to see it for the first time.

and was practically the first opera produced in England. Scenery was, for the first time, employed in a play as distinguished from a masque, and it introduced upon the stage the first Englishwoman (Mrs. Coleman) who ever in our English drama appeared upon it."

Among the composers and actors in *The Siege of Rhodes* was Matthew Locke. He was one of the " old guard " and is mentioned by Samuel Pepys, the diarist, in one of his early entries. He was a remarkable man—very abusive in controversy, which he seemed to love. But he was, undoubtedly, a great musician, and I have learned to value his work much more highly than I once did. He was one of the first—if not *the* first—to completely write an English opera, and his *Psyche* is full of excellent things. He has been credited with the *Macbeth* music, but, among others, Dr. Cummings (no mean judge, and a great student of music of this period) does not allow him this credit, and claims the work as an early specimen of Henry Purcell. I confess I do not see in the *Macbeth* music the hand of Locke. I have performed most of his *Psyche* and also a remarkable dialogue by Locke on the death of Lord Sandwich, which seems to me to very greatly differ in distinction and dramatic feeling from the *Macbeth* music. He contributed the chief instrumental music to a version of *The Tempest* produced as an opera in 1674. But before turning our attention to the important position of it as an opera we must consider *The Tempest* as a play, known as the Davenant-Dryden version, produced in 1667. It contained some songs by various composers and was the production seen by Pepys, and of which he makes some delightful criticisms. Under the date 7th November, 1667, he writes, " The most innocent play that ever I saw, and a curious piece of music is an echo of half sentences, the echo repeating the former half sentence while the man goes on to the latter which is mighty pretty." He

DR. MATTHEW LOCKE

saw it again a little later, and says, " It is very pleasant, only the seaman's part a little too tedious." Then, much later, he sees it again, and says: " Which I have often seen but yet was pleased again, and shall be again to see it. It is full of variety." Still later on he writes, " Which still pleases me mightily. . . ." The piece of music which Pepys so accurately described, and which he got Banister, the composer of the item, to copy down for him, is fortunately preserved.

Of course, this duet between Ariel and Ferdinand is an addition to Shakespeare's *Tempest*. And this is what we have to consider with most of the music which follows. The alteration of Shakespeare's plays after the Restoration is a subject which has given rise to much controversy and much denunciation of the poets who undertook this work. This matter was commented upon a good many years ago by Professor Edward Taylor, in one of his Gresham lectures, and his remarks are worth quoting: " When the theatres re-opened at the period of the Restoration it seemed taken for granted that the plays of Shakespeare were unfit for representation until they had received both corrections and additions from the dramatists of that time. To this employment Dryden, Tate, Otway and Cibber especially addressed themselves, and their example was followed by other writers of more slender literary pretensions. Had they contented themselves with a few judicious retrenchments their labour would have been well bestowed, but in venturing to mix up their own base metal with the pure gold of Shakespeare they have only perpetuated an instance of their own temerity and folly."

This is rather strong language, and later writers take a different view of the matter. Mr. Mostyn Summers, in his excellent book *Shakespearean Adaptations*, puts the matter in a different and—to me—a more consistent light. He says, " It is not through any lack of appreciation of Shakespeare's genius that the plays have been altered and modified. The dramatists of the reign of Charles II. yield to none in their admiration for Shakespeare. Shadwell speaks of the inimitable hand of Shakespeare'" (see Preface to *Timon of Athens*). "It must be added," he says, " I have made it a play." Dryden also declares in the Prologue to *The Tempest* (1670):

> But Shakespeare's magick could not copy'd be,
> Within that circle none durst walk but he.

Mr. Summers also very pertinently says, "The picture stage had replaced the platform stage, and the picture stage necessitated the revision of plays which were written for another method of representation."

So far as music is concerned we are the gainers, for the new versions of the plays, and of course the operatic versions, called for much more music, and that music of a more elaborate character.

The echo song, so admired by Pepys, is a very effective item on the stage: Ariel, behind the scenes (or, in the machines, as the old stage direction has it), echoing the last words of Ferdinand at the front of the stage.

It is a good example of Banister's skill, being written in canon form, and the echoing and overlapping of the phrases is very cleverly managed. (See page 81 of Appendix.)

CHAPTER VII

THE PLAYS (*continued*)

THE other songs included in the play are difficult to identify. Mr. Barclay Squire has made a very close study of the matter and thinks the songs which appear in the original were not in Shadwell's version. It seems pretty certain that Humfrey's " Where the bee sucks " was not, for Pepys says of Humfrey in November 1667, " lately returned from France," so that it is most unlikely he had contributed " Where the bee sucks." It is possible that the songs used in the play were the original settings by R. Johnson, and that Banister, besides the Echo duet, contributed "Come unto these yellow sands." Banister was a very prominent musician, at one time Master of the King's Band. He was supplanted by Grabu, a Frenchman, and the historians have told us that the reason was he had the temerity to tell the king that he preferred English violins (*i.e.* players) to Frenchmen! Pepys tells us, under date 20th February, 1666, " They talk how the King's violin, Banister, is mad that a Frenchman is come to be chief of some part of the King's musique."

As a matter of fact it transpires that Banister was not dismissed for his patriotic sentiments, but because it was found he omitted to make certain payments to the band! Charles II. seems to have behaved quite fairly to him and the complaint of the injured members of the band was properly investigated, with the result that Banister lost his post.

A point of interest about Banister is that he appears to have started the first public concerts in England. Roger North tells us, " He procured a large room in Whitefryers, near the Temple back gate, and made a large raised box

HERE LYETH Y BODY OF
M IOHN BANESTER
WHO DEPARTED THIS LIFE
Y 3" OF OCTOBER IN Y
YEARE 1679

for the musicians, whose modesty required curtaines. The room was rounded with seats and small tables, alehouse fashion. One shilling was the price, and call for what you pleased; there was very good musick, for Banister found means to procure the best hands in towne and some voices

[NOTE.—The tablet spells the name Banester, but all the contemporary records of the composer spell it Banister.]

to come and perform there, and there wanted no variety of humour, for Banister himself (*inter alia*) did wonders upon a flageolet to a thro' bass, and the several masters had their solos. This continued full one winter, and more I remember not."

He seems to have outlived his fault in connection with the King's Band, and there is a small tablet to his memory in the Cloisters of Westminster Abbey.

The setting of " Where the bee sucks " which Humfrey contributed to the opera is very much more modern than the setting by Johnson. It has a delightful change of key at the words " Merrily, merrily shall I live now," but there is one noticeable alteration in the words of this lyric, possibly made by Dryden. Instead of " On the bat's back " we find " On the swallow's wings I fly." This is one of the very sad alterations which have been made in this beautiful song. This line is not un-Shakespearean, for we find, " True hope is swift, and flies with swallow's wings." But the alteration is to be deplored, and still more the constant alteration of the first line, " Where the bee sucks, there *lurk* I." This is what Arne set, and even Sir Arthur Sullivan made the same error in his beautiful setting. And we constantly find the word " summer " changed to " sunset," a change made by Theobald in a work entitled *Shakespeare Restored*, published in 1726. In Charles Knight's well-known edition I find the following comment, " Warburton supports the old reading very ingeniously. The roughness of winter is represented by Shakespeare as disagreeable to fairies and such-like delicate spirits, who, on this account, constantly follow summer. Was not this then the most agreeable circumstance of Ariel's new-recovered liberty, that he could now avoid winter and follow summer quite round the world? "

This is, no doubt, the real sentiment of the words. We find the same idea in Milton's *Comus*.

It is to be hoped that educated vocalists will accept Shakespeare's words, and not travesty this lovely song; but it is very difficult to get rid of such errors. I heard, quite lately, a distinguished vocalist sing not only " there lurk I," but actually, instead of " there I couch," she sang " there I *crouch*." Evidently she imagined she was lurking and crouching to capture the unfortunate bee when it left its flowery bower!

Humfrey, as is well known, was sent to study with Lully in Paris by Charles II., and we meet with him in Pepys' *Diary* on his return. He seems to have had a good opinion of himself, and a rather bad one of some of his musical contemporaries. Pepys records some of his remarks under date 15th November, 1667:

Home, and there I found, as I expected, Mr. Cæsar and little Pelham Humfreys, lately returned from France and an absolute monsieur, as full of form and confidence and vanity, and disparages everything and everybody's skill but his own. But to hear how he laughs at all the King's music here, as Blagrave and others, that they cannot keep time nor tune, nor understand anything, and " Grebus " the Frenchman, the King's Master of the Music, how he understands nothing, nor can play on any instrument and so cannot compose, and that he will give him a lift out of his place, and that he and the King are mighty great!

Alas! poor fellow, he did not live long, dying at the early age of twenty-seven—only seven years after he had expressed so poor an opinion of his brother musicians. But he had considerable influence on English music.

He had the honour of teaching Purcell as a Chapel Royal boy, and we may suppose influenced him not a little. He seems to have inclined to dramatic writing, for he also set a version of the " Willo Willo " song. But a more important contribution of his has lately been discovered in the Library of the Conservatoire at Paris. This is the music for Shadwell's operatic version of *The Tempest*, produced in 1674. It must have been one of Humfrey's latest efforts, for he died in that same year (1674), and is buried in the Cloisters of Westminster Abbey.

A recent writer has said, " Of all Shakespeare's plays there appear to have been none which was revised more often and which ever drew more crowded houses than *The Tempest*."

INTERIOR OF WREN'S THEATRE
(DORSET GARDENS, 1674)

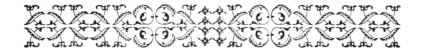

CHAPTER VIII

SHADWELL'S operatic version of *The Tempest* was performed at Dorset Gardens in 1674. This was a new theatre, designed by Wren. It was, apparently, a large and beautiful structure, and views of both exterior and interior have, fortunately, been preserved, and are here reproduced. From the 1673 Quarto of the libretto we have a very complete description of the stage :

> The Front of the Stage is open'd, and the Band of 24 Violins, with the Harpsicals and Theorbo's which accompany the Voices are plac'd between the Pit and the Stage. While the Overture is playing the Curtain rises, and discovers a new Frontispiece, joyn'd to the great Pilasters, on each side of the Stage. This Frontispiece is a noble Arch, supported by large wreathed Columns of the Corinthian Order; the wreathings of the Columns are beautifi'd with Roses wound round them, and several Cupids flying about them. On the Cornice, just over the Capitals, sits on either side a Figure, with a Trumpet in one hand, and a Palm in the other, representing Fame. A little farther on the same Cornice, on each side of a Compass-pediment, lie a Lion and a Unicorn, the Supporters of the Royal Arms of England. In the middle of the Arch are several Angels, holding the King's Arms, as if they were placing them in the midst of that Compass-pediment. Behind this is the Scene, which represents a thick Cloudy Sky, a very Rocky Coast, and a Tempestuous Sea in perpetual Agitation. This Tempest (suppos'd to be rais'd by Magick) has many dreadful Objects in it, as several Spirits in horrid shapes flying down among the Sailers, then rising and crossing in the Air. And when the Ship is sinking, the whole House is darken'd and a shower of Fire falls upon 'em. This is

accompanied with Lightening, and several Claps of Thunder, to the end of the Storm.

The libretto was based upon the Davenant-Dryden version. It was thus noticed by Downes :

The Tempest, or Inchanted Island, made into an opera by Mr. Shadwell, having all new in it, as scenery, machines, particularly one scene painted with myriads of ariel spirits, and another flying away with a table furnished with fruits, sweetmeats and all sorts of viands, just when Duke Trinculo and his companions were going to dinner, all things performed in it so absolutely well that not any succeeding opera got more money.

The lyrics inserted in the 1667 play were included in the opera, including the Echo duet of Banister and his " Come unto these yellow sands." Banister also furnished " Full fathom five," which probably appeared in the 1667 play. It is not nearly so good as the original setting. " Where the bee sucks " was not the only contribution by Humfrey. The addition of a terminal masque, in which Neptune, Amphitrite, Oceanus and Tethys appear, was an important feature of the opera, and there was music for this masque and for a very elaborate Act II., where three devils sing, at first under the stage and later on are joined on the stage by Pride, Fraud, Rapine and Murder—all singing characters. The music for Act II. and the concluding masque, composed by Pelham Humfrey, has lately fortunately been discovered in the Library of the Paris Conservatoire. It is in MS. and has apparently never been printed.

I have had the opportunity of producing this interesting find at some of my lectures. There is no orchestral accompaniment—only the vocal parts (solos and short three-part choruses) and the bass. There is much of real dramatic music in this work—the best part of it in the masque: where the music for Neptune is particularly effective.

Another very important contribution was a fine song at the end of Act II., " Arise, ye subterranean winds." This was contributed by an Italian composer resident in this country, Pietro Reggio. It is much more vocal and modern in style than the music of Locke or Humfrey. Indeed, it appears to me to be superior to Purcell's setting of these words, being entirely free from long-winded "divisions," *i.e.* florid passages. It was, fortunately, published by the composer in a volume of songs. Shadwell evidently had a high opinion of Reggio and pays him some nice compliments in a poetical preface to this volume, which is worth quoting:

SHADWELL'S PREFACE TO PIETRO REGGIO'S BOOK OF SONGS

If I could write with a Poetic fire
Equal to thine in Musick, I'd admire
And praise thee fully: now my verse will be
Short of Thy merit, as I short of Thee.

.   .   .   .   .   .

Thy worth and skill great Jenkins lov'd and knew,
The worthiest master of my youthful days,
Whom Thou so justly honor'st with thy Praise.
But the Pretenders of this Quacking age
Who with their ditties plague the Town and Stage,
If their dull notes will but the numbers fit
Ne'er mind the Poet's spirit or his wit.
But think all's done if it be done by rule
Though one may write true Grammar like a Fool;
Still in their Beaten Road they troll along,
And make alike the sad and cheerful Song.
The Pastoral and the Warlike are the same,
The Dirge and Triumph differ but in Name.
Such their Performance is: nay, not so good.
A Funeral Song they chant with cheerful mood,
And sigh and languish in a drunken Ode,

H

In Martial Ones they're soft, in Am'rous rough,
And never think they shake and grace enough.

. . . . . .

We cannot call this singing, but a noise,
Not gracing, but a Jogging of the Voice.

This " Jenkins " that Shadwell alludes to as " the
worthiest master of my youthful days " was a very celebrated and long-lived composer. He wrote a great deal
of music—many fancies for strings and much vocal music,
both sacred and secular. He is, however, really only known
now as the composer of the little round, " A boat, a boat
unto the ferry." He is mentioned with great respect by
Roger North, who was also his pupil. Jenkins was born
in 1597, and North died in 1734, so master and pupil
covered many years. Jenkins lived in the Wodehouse family,
at Kimberley in Norfolk, and is buried there. The following
is the somewhat original epitaph on his gravestone:

Under this stone rare Jenkyns lye,
The master of the musick art,
Whom from the earth, the God on high,
Called up to him, to bear his part.
Aged 86, October 27,
In Anno 78 he went to Heaven.

As we have Locke's instrumental music complete, the
songs by Humfrey, Banister and Reggio, the Echo duet,
beloved by Pepys, the recently discovered music for Act II.
and the concluding masque by Humfrey, we are able to
form a tolerably correct notion of this most interesting
work. One would like to see it all in print.

Shadwell wrote a Prologue to this opera, beginning:

We, as the fathers of the stage have said,
To treat you here a vast expense have made.

And the Epilogue mentions the machines, singers and dancers:

> We have machines to some perfection brought,
> And above thirty warbling voices gott,
> Many a god and godess you will hear,
> And we have singing, dancing, devils here.
> Such devils, and such gods, are very dear!

The singers were from the Chapel Royal. In the Lord Chamberlain's accounts it is recorded on 11th May, 1674, that "it is His Majesty's pleasure that Mr. Thomas and Mr. Hart or any other men and boys belonging to His Majesty's Chappel Royal that sing in *The Tempest* at His Royal Highness's Theatre do remain in town all the week during His Majesty's absence from Whitehall, to perform that service." On Saturdays, however, they had to go to Windsor, since the king was in residence at the Castle, for the Sunday services. They were allowed to return to London on Mondays "if there be occasion for them."

Locke's instrumental music is of considerable importance. It consists largely of dance forms, such as the galliard, gavot and saraband, a curious piece called a "lilk," and a particularly interesting " curtain tune "—this is an attempt to suggest the storm and shipwreck. It opens with a soft, smooth progression, suggestive of a " calm sea and prosperous voyage," becoming louder by degrees and introducing elaborate and rapid passages for the various instruments. One curious musical term used is " violent "; probably we should now write " agitato." The music becomes softer and slower by degrees, and the finale is a calm. This is an early specimen of programme music and decidedly effective. Other numbers of Locke's work include a corant and martial jig, and the audience disperses to the music of a clever canon, " 4 in 2," as it is called. Altogether it is a matter to rejoice at that we have so good an example of music written for the stage at this important period in the development of opera.

The recovery of Humfrey's music written for this opera is a very happy fact. He lived too short a life to have made a very great name, and yet he is a remarkable figure in the music of Restoration times; and the few songs which we know and also some of his Church music are proofs of his talent.[1] But *The Tempest* music is a very striking testimony to his powers. And it has peculiar interest from the fact that his great pupil, Henry Purcell, certainly had knowledge of it. In his own setting of *The Tempest* we are often reminded of Humfrey's music. The opening song in Purcell's has a great resemblance to the opening of Humfrey's; the time-measure is the same, though, of course, this is suggested by the rhythm of the words. Later on, in a song for Æolus, "To your prisons below, down, down ye shall go," though the words are slightly altered, the phrase of five bars of music is really the same in Purcell as we find in Humfrey.

The best part of Humfrey's setting is a duet between Neptune and Amphitrite.

The early death of Humfrey was, undoubtedly, a great loss to our English school of operatic music, only equalled by the early death of his great pupil, Purcell.

[1] The Grand Chant, so well known to Church musicians, is by Humfrey.

HENRY PURCELL

CHAPTER IX

PURCELL'S setting of *The Tempest* is, perhaps, the best known of all his operatic work. The play itself has always had great attraction for the public, and this has been the case also with the operatic version. I have already considered at some length Shadwell's version, with its music by Locke, Banister, Humfrey and Reggio, and Purcell's setting demands equal consideration. The story of the Restoration version of Shakespeare's *Tempest* (as Mr. Barclay Squire writes) is curiously intricate, and has been fully told by Mr. W. J. Lawrence in *The Elizabethan Playhouse* (1912), and by Mr. Squire himself.

The libretto set by Purcell follows very closely Shadwell's version, and is, of course, very different in many respects from Shakespeare's play. " Come unto these yellow sands " is rather mutilated so far as words go.

Shakespeare wrote:

> Hark! hark! I hear
> The strain of strutting chanticleer
> Cry, Cock-a-doodle-do.

But the version Purcell set omits the last line, and ends baldly with " strutting chanticleer."

" Where the bee sucks " does not appear, but the song " Arise, ye subterranean winds " (already set to music by Reggio) is a very elaborate composition and a great favourite with bass vocalists to this day.

Purcell's choruses are elaborate and dramatic. An

interesting fact is that some of the sentiments and curses of the devils—much about the cruelty and tyranny of kings—are omitted in Purcell's setting, though they appear in Humfrey's.

Certain numbers of this setting are among the most popular examples from Purcell; " Come unto these yellow sands " and " Full fathom five " are in the repertoire of every choral society. But, on the whole, I do not think the music of this opera is as good as most of the music we find in a later opera by Purcell, entitled *The Fairy Queen*, founded on Shakespeare's *Midsummer Night's Dream*. This I shall now consider.

" THE FAIRY QUEEN " (PURCELL)

This opera is particularly interesting to all lovers of Shakespeare. Although the libretto is a travesty of Shakespeare and does not provide a single line of the poet's verse to be set to music, yet it is founded so much on Shakespeare's play and has so many scenes requiring music of a special fairy-like character, that it seems to have drawn from Purcell some of the best examples of his dramatic genius. The instrumental numbers are numerous and often exceedingly effective. It is curious how often Purcell chooses to set himself a difficult task by writing in what is called " strict canon," and often by using a ground-bass. In the use of canonic effects he imitates Locke, who used the same form in *Psyche*. There is much really comical music. The opening scene in particular, where the drunken poet is tormented by the fairies, is extremely funny. The stuttering of the poet [1] in such passages as " Fi-fi-fill up the bowl," " Tu-tu-turn me round," is truly comic, and the fairy music

---

[1] It is suggested that the poet, with his stammers, may have meant T. D'Urfey, who was known as " Poet Stutter."

light and tuneful. There are some quaint scenes which are not very Shakespearean; one in which swans are seen floating (to a very expressive bit of music), and which suddenly turn into fairies and dance, and are frightened away by four savages (or furies as they are called in one edition of Purcell's work) who suddenly appear and dance an entry. And later on there is another remarkable scene. The stage is suddenly illuminated and discloses a transparent prospect of a Chinese garden. A Chinese man and woman enter and sing a duet, and some monkeys come from behind the trees and dance. Truly Purcell had to write some varied music!

This was the *Midsummer Night's Dream* in 1692. The author of the libretto is not known, but Purcell's music was composed near the end of his short career, and shows clearly how he was influenced by the Italian school. When we compare his music with Locke's *Psyche* we see how greatly English music has been thus influenced.

The score of this work was lost in 1701. A reward of twenty guineas was offered for its recovery, but with no result. By a singular chance Mr. Shedlock, when editing the opera for the Purcell Society and exploring all avenues to find various parts of this opera, found the missing score in the shelter of the Royal Academy of Music. It had been left to the Royal Academy in 1837 by R. J. Stevens, the Gresham Professor of Music (elected 1801), organist of the Temple and Charterhouse, but until its fortunate discovery by Mr. Shedlock no one seems to have been aware of the location of the lost score. Stevens, no doubt, obtained it from Savage (whose name is on the inside of the score), and Savage was a pupil of Pepusch, who was for several years at the beginning of the eighteenth century connected with the Theatre Royal, Drury Lane, and we are told was an enthusiastic "collector of manuscripts"! This seems to be the history of the lost score.

Stevens probably valued the MS. very highly and may not have known that it had been lost. He was a very prolific writer of glees—as they were called—but which were often accompanied and more like modern part-songs, and he set beautifully many of Shakespeare's lyrics which are constantly sung by choral societies. These include " Ye spotted snakes," " Crabbed age and youth," " Blow, blow, thou winter wind," " Sigh no more, ladies," and others. It is said he was prompted to set these words by Alderman Birch, who was a confectioner living in Cornhill, and the founder of the present firm of Ring and Brymer who occupy Birch's old shop. Alderman Birch was a great lover of Shakespeare. He ultimately became Lord Mayor of London, and, no doubt, Stevens owed his nomination to be Gresham Professor to his old friend and collaborator, the Lord Mayor. The Gresham Trust is administered by a joint committee of the Corporation and the Mercers Company, and the Lord Mayor is chairman.

This old lover of Shakespeare did a service in inducing Stevens to set so many of Shakespeare's lyrics, and deserves to be mentioned in these pages.

This opera has quite lately been performed at Cambridge with much success.

The Preface to the work (I suppose by its anonymous author) is evidence of the great desire among authors and composers to establish firmly opera in England. After calling attention to the popularity of the opera in Italy and France and noticing that " the noble Venetians set 'em out at their own cost," the writer says, " If an opera were established here by the Favour of the Nobility and Gentry of England I may modestly conclude it would be some advantage to London, considering what a sum we must yearly lay out among Tradesmen for the following out so great a work."

His comment upon the work of Sir William Davenant in promoting opera is exceedingly interesting:

That Sir William Davenant's *Siege of Rhodes* was the first opera we ever had in England no man could deny. 'Tis true the *Siege of Rhodes* wanted the ornaments of machines, which they value themselves so much upon in Italy, and the dancing, which they have in such perfection in France. That he design'd this if his first attempt met with the encouragement it deserv'd will appear from these lines in his Prologue:

> " Ah Mony, Mony! if the wits would dress
> With ornaments the present face of peace:
> And to our Poet half that Treasure spare
> Which Faction gets from Fools to furnish War,
> Then the Contracted Scene should wider be
> And move by greater Engines; till you see
> (While you securely sit) fierce armies meet
> And raging seas disperse a fighting fleet."

He concludes:

That a few private persons should venture on so expensive a work as an opera, when none but princes or states exhibit 'em abroad, I hope is no dishonour to our nation. If this happens to please we cannot necessarily propose to ourselves any great advantage, considering the mighty charge in setting it out and the extraordinary expense that attends it every day 'tis represented. If it deserves their favour, if they are satisfied, we venture boldly, doing all we can to please 'em. We hope the English are too generous not to encourage so great an undertaking.

It is said the opera appeared without any mention of the author or the composer. But it certainly seems as if Purcell was quite alive to the opportunity and to the attraction of the libretto, and his music is among the best examples of his fancy and genius.

I

A FACSIMILE OF THE PAGE IN PEPYS' MS. BOOK

CHAPTER X

HAMLET'S SOLILOQUY

THE last specimen of Shakespearean music which I am to consider is, I think, somewhat unique, and so far unknown, except to those who have attended some of my lectures. It is a setting of the celebrated soliloquy in *Hamlet*. I do not know of any other musical setting of this splendid passage. I was fortunate enough to notice it when looking over Pepys' musical manuscripts in the Library of Magdalene College. The soliloquy is alluded to once in Pepys' *Diary*. On 13th March, 1664, we read, " Spent all the afternoon with my wife indoors and getting a speech out of *Hamlet*, ' To bee or not to bee,' without book."

This seems to refer to the words only, or Pepys might mean the music also, although I doubt his being able to get this " without book," but the entry shows his appreciation of the passage.

The question who composed the music is a little difficult. The setting is found in a large volume of manuscript music, beautifully bound, and with a title page which runs as follows:

SONGS AND OTHER COMPOSITIONS
LIGHT, GRAVE AND SACRED
FOR A
SINGLE VOICE
ADJUSTED TO THE PARTICULAR COMPASS OF MINE
WITH A THORO' BASS ON YE GUITAR
BY
CESARE MORELLI.

A label on the book bears the date of 1693.

There is a complete index to the music, and several items are bracketed together under the name of Morelli.

Morelli does not appear in the *Diary*. He was an Italian in the service of a nobleman at Lisbon. He was sent to Pepys in 1675 by his friend Mr. Hill, and was described as having a most admirable voice and singing rarely to his theorbo and with great skill. Pepys took him into his service, paying him £30 a year with his lodging and entertainment.

Morelli evidently rendered his employer great assistance in his musical studies, but in 1678 Pepys requested him to move from his house and to live at Brentwood, as Morelli was a Roman Catholic and his presence in Pepys' house brought an accusation of Pepys being also a Roman Catholic. But though Morelli was no longer in the house Pepys corresponded, and consulted with him on musical matters. In September 1679 he writes to him that he wished Morelli were present, " for then I would have consulted with you about the table which you have given me for the guitar, and as I would be glad to improve that little knowledge as far as I could, to making myself capable by the help of your table of playing a bass continuo."

A few years later Morelli returned to the Continent, and in 1686 wrote to Pepys to ask for a place in the Chapel Royal choir. We have no record of his appointment.

I cannot believe Morelli composed this song, although his name appears in the index to the volume. But it seems to me that the real explanation is that Pepys got some good composer to set it, and that Morelli " adjusted it to the particular compass " of Pepys' voice and added a guitar accompaniment. It is interesting to find the guitar table which Pepys mentions

SAMUEL PEPYS

inserted inside the cover of this volume. I give a facsimile,[1] p. 73.

Now, who could have composed it?

After many hearings and much consideration, and also comparing it with other compositions (notably a dialogue on the death of Lord Sandwich) by Matthew Locke, I have come to the conclusion that he is the composer. Locke was a friend of Pepys, mentioned in the early pages of the *Diary* (February 1659–60), and would be a very likely man for Pepys to employ to set the words. Pepys saw *Hamlet* in 1661 and tells us, " Betterton did the Prince's part beyond imagination." He also saw it on two other occasions in the same year. Two years later he again saw it and remarks, " giving us fresh reason never to think enough of Betterton." And yet, once more, in 1688 he is still " mightily pleased with it, but above all with Betterton, *the best part* I believe *that ever man acted!* "

It is quite reasonable to conclude that Pepys got this fine passage set to music during these years, and long before he came to know Morelli. And if this is so, it makes this setting specially interesting. The musician who set it no doubt saw Betterton in the part, and we are told, " The character of Hamlet was one of Betterton's masterpieces. Downe tells us that he was taught by Davenant how the part was acted by Taylor of the Blackfriars, *who was instructed by Shakespeare himself.*"

Sir Sidney Lee suggested that so the composer may have caught some of the Shakespearean tradition, and I think this is very likely. There is one little point about which I may venture a few words. The composer has set the opening words in a very dramatic way, as a sort of recitative and detached from the rest of the setting, and he

---

[1] Although the book in which this table appears is dated 1693, yet we see that Pepys had this table from Morelli in 1679.

makes a striking variety in the text: " To be, or not to be, *that's* the question." (This is followed by three bars of symphony before the words "Whether 't be¹ nobler.") "That's the question " is substituted for " that is the question."

Did Betterton declaim it so? Pepys was so very particular and minute in his criticisms that I do not believe he would have accepted this version unless he had heard it so given by Betterton. If Locke set it to music he, no doubt, put a figured bass—this, of course, Morelli had to discard when he arranged it for his guitar, of which he was such a master.

As we have no other copy I have been obliged to add an accompaniment of my own. When this soliloquy is sung by a vocalist of real dramatic feeling it never fails to make a profound impression. Indeed, many ardent Shakespearean students have told me the musical setting greatly intensifies the significance of the splendid text.²

The words differ in several places from the First Folio. I have kept strictly to the text as it appears in the manuscript, and possibly Shakespearean scholars will be able to identify the source from which Pepys' composer got it. So far as the music is concerned I have made no alteration of the melody. I have added a short symphony to introduce it, and it appears (for the first time in print) in the Appendix.

I give the text of Pepys' version.

---

¹ " 't be " is in Pepys, and not " 'tis."

² It is also particularly interesting in the fact that, so far as I know, it is the earliest setting of any of Shakespeare's text, *i.e.* with the exception of the songs in the plays and three madrigals for the words from the *Passionate Pilgrim.*

BETTERTON AS "HAMLET"

HAMLET'S SOLILOQUY

Act III. Scene i.

To be; or not to be; that's the Question.
   Whether 't be nobler in the mind; to suffer
the slings and arrows of outragious fortune;
or to take arms against a sea of troubles,
and by opposing, end them?
                   To die; to sleep;
Noe more. And by a sleep, to say wee end
the Heartake, and the thousand nat'rall shocks
that flesh is heir to, is a consummation
devoutly to be wish'd. To die; to sleep.
To sleep; perchance to dream; I; there's the rubb.
For in that sleep of death, what dreams may come;
When wee have shuffl'd off this mortall Coyle,
Must give us Pause.   There's the respect,
that makes Calamity of so Long Life.
For who would bear, the whipps and scorns of Time,
the Oppressour's wrong, the poor man's Contumelye,
the pangs of despis'd Love, the Law's delays,
The Insolence of Office, and the spurns
that patient Meritt of the unworthy takes,
When hee himself might his Quietus make,
With a bare Bodkin?
             Who would these fardles bear,
to groan and sweat under a weary Life,
but that the dread of something after death,
that undiscover'd Country, from whose Borne
no Traveller return's, puzzles the will,
and makes us rather bear, those Ills wee have,
than flie to others, that wee know not of?
   Thus, Conscience makes Cowards of us all;
and thus, the native Hue of Resolution,
is sickly'd o're with the pale Caste of Thought;
And Enterprizes of greatest Pith and Moment,
with this reguard, their Currents turn awry,
And loose the name of Action.

With this setting of one of the finest passages in Shakespeare I close my little survey of the seventeenth-century music. The eighteenth century is almost a blank as regards worthy music to Shakespeare. Arne, with his " Where the bee sucks," is the most outstanding figure, and we have a few pleasant part-songs and glees by nineteenth-century composers. The twentieth century has more to its credit, and Shakespeare has been drawn upon by opera and orchestral composers and song writers, in many cases with signal success. But to embark on a summary of these recent contributions is beyond my power. I hope what I have written of the early settings of the poet's words will be acceptable to lovers of Shakespeare, as a small tribute from one who has found much relaxation in this pleasant task.

The Notes upon each String of ye Guitar apply'd to those on the Scale.

Gam-ut.	A-Re.	B-Mi-ut.	C-Fa-ut.		D-Sol-Re.		E-La-Mi-ut.	F-Fa-ut.		G-Sol-RE-ut.	Strings
d.	f	h.	i.	k.	t.		m.	b.	c	i.	1st.
k.	g.	a.	b.	c.	d.		e.	g.	h.	l.	2.
b.	d.	e.	f.	g.	h.		i.	q.	m.	d.	3.
g.	h.	k.	k.	m.	a.		k.	d.	e.	f.	4.
m.	a.	c.	d.	e.	f.		g.	c.	k.	k.	5.
Sol.	La.	Mi.	Fa.		Sol.		La.	Fa.		Sol.	

FROM PEPYS' MS. BOOK IN MAGDALENE COLLEGE LIBRARY

MUSICAL APPENDIX

MUSICAL APPENDIX

O MISTRESSE MINE

(With Morley's original Harmony for the Citterne and Pandora)

From Morley's *Consort Lesson*, 1599.

77

sweet - ing,   Jour - neys end   in . .   lov - ers

meet - ing, Ev - - 'ry wise man's son doth know.

GREENSLEEVES

(The generally accepted Version)

A - las, my love, you do me wrong to cast me off dis -
- cour - teous - ly, And I have lov - ed you so long, de -
- light - ing in your com - pan - y. Green - sleeves was
all my joy, Green - sleeves was my de - light,
Green-sleeves was my heart of gold, and who but my La - dy Green-sleeves.

GREENSLEEVES

The Version given by Cobbold in his *Humorous Fancy or New Fashions*

(Probably about 1610.)

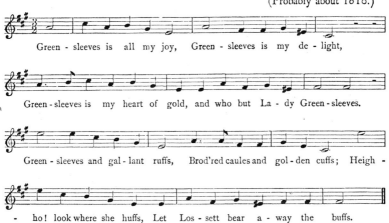

Green - sleeves is all my joy, Green - sleeves is my de - light,
Green - sleeves is my heart of gold, and who but La - dy Green - sleeves.
Green - sleeves and gal - lant ruffs, Brod'red caules and gol - den cuffs; Heigh -
- ho! look where she huffs, Let Los - sett bear a - way the buffs.

PEG O' RAMSEY

Cobbold's Version   (1610?)

Lit - tle Peg o' Ram - sey with the yel - low hair, And could'st thou

greet if I were dead? Mar - ry would I seare; And

could'st thou greet if I were dead? Mar - ry would I seare.

WHOOP! DO ME NO HARM, GOOD MAN

(Song mentioned in Shakespeare's *Winter's Tale* as part of the wares of Autolycus
the Pedlar.)

Andante.

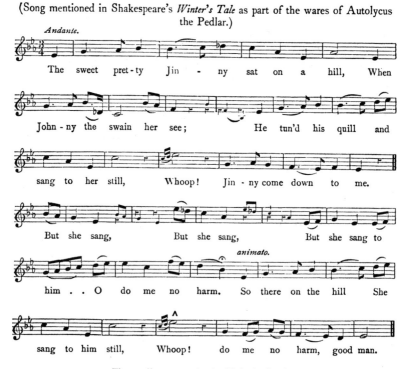

The sweet pret - ty Jin - ny sat on a hill, When

John - ny the swain her see; He tun'd his quill and

sang to her still, Whoop! Jin - ny come down to me.

But she sang, But she sang, But she sang to

him . . O do me no harm. So there on the hill She

animato.

sang to him still, Whoop! do me no harm, good man.

The small notes are for the Viola da Gamba.

ECHO DUET

(From Shadwell's version of *The Tempest*)

store for . . thee some strange fe - - li - ci - ty; Fol - low me,

fol - low me, and thou shalt see : Fol-low me, fol - low me, and thou shalt see.

* If the singer turns round and sings in the opposite direction the effect of greater distance will be attained. The accompaniment must be exceedingly light, and for the last four bars the Right Hand part may be omitted.

TO BE; OR NOT TO BE;

Accompaniment
added by Sir F. Bridge.

Hamlet's Soliloquy
Act III, Scene i

From the original MS.
in the Pepysian Library.

* Being a Recit. the singer would probably sing *E*.

With this re - gard their cur-rents turn a - wry, And

loose the name of Ac - tion.

* The vocalist would probably sing *E* in the style of a Recitative.

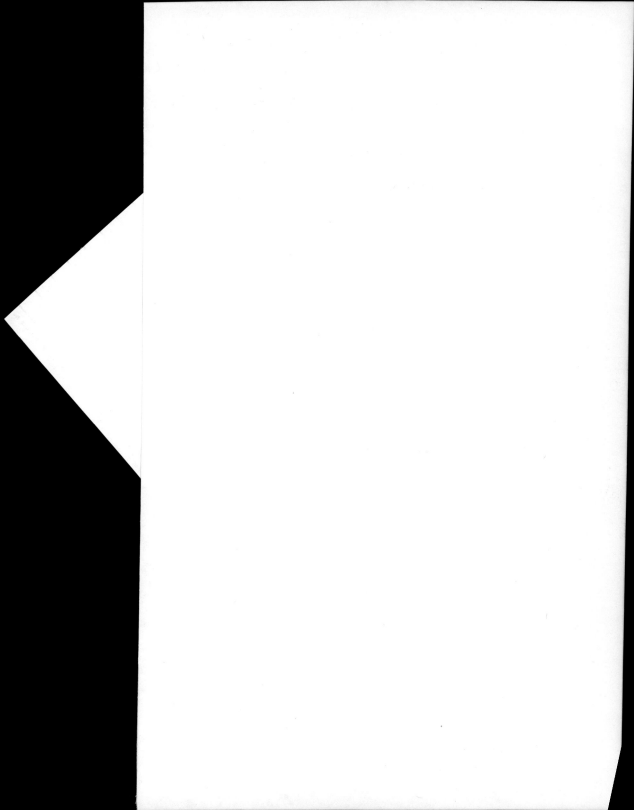

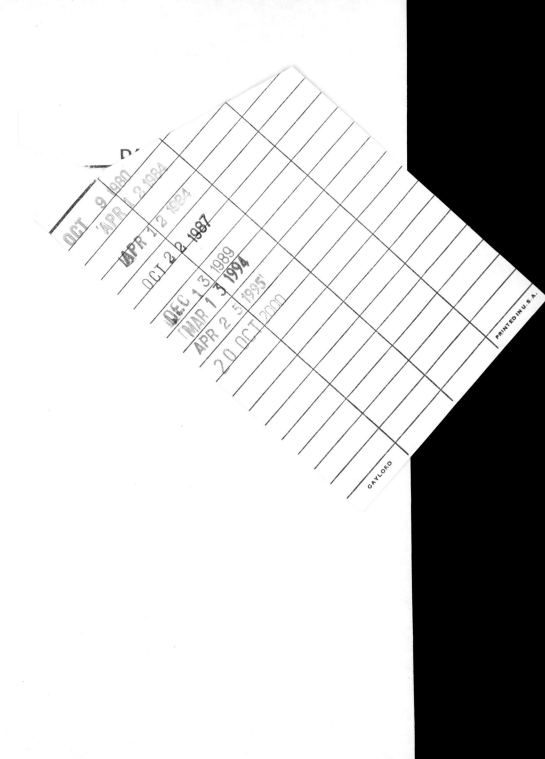